THINGS I WANTED
MY GRANDSONS TO KNOW
before I Leave

KENN STOBBE

Things I Wanted My Grandsons to Know before I Leave

Paperback ISBN: 978-1-63812-763-5
Ebook ISBN: 978-1-63812-764-2

Published by Paper Leaf Agency   08/17/2023

Paper Leaf Agency
888-208-0170
admin@paperleafagency.com

Why This Book Was Written

We all build wisdom in our life's journeys. As we age, though, it can be difficult to determine how and when to pass that knowledge to loved ones.

My wife and I were blessed with our two grandsons when I was already in the winter of my life and I feared I would not live long enough to share with them those things I thought were important for them to know. I decided books, written to them, would be the perfect solution. Thus I wrote "Things I Wanted My Grandson To Know Before I Leave", (Chapter 1) and "Things I Wanted My Grandsons To Know Before I Leave" (Chapter2).

In my two books (Chapters 1 & 2), I offer my two grandsons a collection of quotes, sayings, snippets, and examinations designed to inform, delight, and inspire. By sharing wisdom I have gleaned from my decades on this Earth, I challenge my grandsons to live successful, God-centered lives, and offer a heartfelt approach to living an authentic life. Entries range from funny, to sincere, to profound.

As a Nebraskan who has indulged in the pleasures of a simple, honest and hardworking existence alongside my wife, Jan, I have a deep sense of human nature. I take immense pride in sharing hard-earned lessons with my grandsons as well as readers who will benefit from the unique perspective I have culled from walking my life with Jesus.

Contents

Things I Wanted My Grandson To Know

before I Leave

CHAPTER 1

Written by a loving grandfather for his grandson, *Things I Wanted My Grandson to Know Before I Leave* presents a collection of quotes, sayings, snippets, and observations that author Kenn Stobbe believes helped him to live a successful, God-centered life.

Kenn's grandson was born to his only child, an adopted daughter. The boy became the son the older man never had, he was born when Kenn was already in his sixties. Today, a combination of school, distance, sporting events limits his one on one time to share those things that comprised his moral compass with the boy. Now in his 70's and the winter of his life, Kenn—thinking he would not live long enough to pass any words of wisdom along to his grandson as they were growing up—decided to write them out instead.

His primary objective is to help his grandson live the same type of life he has himself. As part of this collection, Kenn addresses, life, love, common sense, manners, morals, values, and beliefs, with a sprinkling of his own thoughts and opinions. Some of the entries are humorous, while others are more serious and thought-provoking.

Things I Wanted My Grandson to Know Before I Leave offers a heartwarming glimpse into the character and integrity of one man and into the depth of his love for his grandson.

KENN STOBBE is a native Nebraskan. Born, raised, educated and employed, until his retirement, in Nebraska's largest city. An avid outdoorsman, Kenn spent much of his spare time hunting, fishing and enjoying the raw beauty of Nebraska's Sandhills. He admired the cowboy way of life—simple, hardworking, and honest. Over the years he befriended many of the local ranchers and cowboys.

His long time goal was to someday live full time in the rugged cattle country. Dreams do come true, and prayers do get answered. He and his wife, Jan, have one daughter and one grandson and now make their home in ranching country northwest of Burwell, Nebraska, in the beautiful Nebraska Sandhills.

Special Thanks:
To my God for giving me the courage to
speak from my heart and letting me live
in the beautiful Nebraska Sandhills

In memory of
"Missy"
(Kathleen Miles)
1947-2014
Big as the Sky!

Introduction

My dearest Grayson,

I was already an old man when you were born so chances of me being around to tell you these things while you are growing up are pretty slim. From the day you were born I began making a list of old sayings, quotations, snippets, lessons I've learned, beliefs, and observations that I believe helped make me who I am; some I read, others were told to me by friends and loved ones, and still others were my own thoughts. Many made me laugh, and many brought tears to my eyes, but all made me think. I thought all were worth knowing and remembering. You are the son I never had and my aim is to share them with you in hopes they might make you a better person, and your journey through this life just a little easier. Only you, your loved ones and friends will ever know if I hit my mark.

There is a God, one God, and His love for us is unconditional and never ending.

Horses probably buck because they don't like people sittin' on 'em.

Always drink from the creek upstream from the herd.

Not everything on the ground in the corral is dirt.

God made mosquitoes, flies, and sandburs to remind us that we are sinners.

Never try to count your blessings 'cause you'll never be able to count that high. And besides, sometimes you will get a blessing and not even know it.

You can never go wrong with Butter Pecan ice cream.

Grandma doesn't really think the firemen will care if your underwear is clean.

Always try and think before you speak, words can hurt and that hurt lasts far longer than a punch in the nose.

I think bulls spend their entire life in a bad mood.

Choose your words carefully; someday you may have to eat them.

It's far better to let people think you're a fool then to open your mouth and remove all doubt.

BIBLE stands for Basic Instructions Before Leaving Earth.

Sometimes it doesn't matter what you say, but it always matters how you say it.

Crayon marks on the wall will wash off.

When you hurt somebody, it's like driving a nail into a piece of wood, you can remove the nail, but the hole will always be there.

It's okay for men to cry, grandpa does his share.

Tears of joy are far better than tears of sorrow.

Good or bad, like it or not, your heart has a mind all its own. You can tell it what to do but it won't listen at all.

Your heart is big enough to love more than one.

"Love" is probably the most overused word in the entire world.

Human nature makes us always want to be first, but being best is a whole lot better.

Remember, it's hard to start a fire with wet wood.

Never try and drown your sorrows, I learned a long time ago they know how to swim.

Don't put the key to your happiness in someone else's pocket; keep it in your own.

Loving your grandma and loving Butter Pecan Ice Cream are not the same.

Worry is like riding a rocking horse; it passes the time, but doesn't take you anywhere.

Anger serves no useful purpose.

Being a cowboy isn't a state of mind, it's a way of life.

If something doesn't look like it's worth the effort, it probably isn't.

Sometimes being silent may be your best answer.

Arguments and fights only prove who's louder or stronger, not who's right or wrong. Sometimes it's real hard, but always try and avoid both.

Walking away from a fight does not mean you're a coward. But if a fight is absolutely unavoidable, don't throw the first punch but do your darnedest to throw the last.

When it comes to horses, admire the big one, but saddle the small one.

Be willing to defend those who can't defend themselves.

It's hard to put your foot in your mouth if it's shut.

If you sleep 8 hours every day, you will have missed 1/3 of your entire life.

We are not born with real contentment, we must learn it.

I guess it's always better to be a "has been" than a "never was".

The hardest thing you will have to do in life is love your neighbor as yourself.

If you always speak kind words, nobody will resent them.

Big or small, all blessings come from God, and like you, He likes to hear "Thank You" now and then too.

It is far better to make dust than to eat dust.

There is a big difference between friends and acquaintances, acquaintances will come and go but true friends last forever.

It's okay to remember past loves, they've helped make you who you are.

Always remember your word is your honor.

Giving credit where credit is due ain't always easy, but it's the right thing to do.

Try and remember your bad decisions, they make for great stories around the campfire.

Never go into anything if you don't know the way out.

All blessings are really presents from God but He doesn't wrap them in shiny paper and ribbons, so sometimes they're hard to recognize.

Don't make promises you know you will have a hard time keepin'.

Good morals and good values are worth far more and will last far longer than money and a new pick-up.

A good friend is someone who laughs at your jokes even when they're not funny.

Be forthright and honest is all your business dealings, your handshake is your bond.

There's only two things you'll find on the back of a bull, fools and flies.

Your life will be a lot more enjoyable if you choose friends that share your morals and values. Your church is a great place to find 'em.

It's perfectly fine to say you made a mistake and even better if you learn from it. Take notice of the mistakes others make and learn from them too.

Practice saying "I'm sorry" you will say it often during your life time.

Finishing last is far better than not finishing at all.

It's one thing to know the right thing to do, the hard part is doin' it.

A sure sign of manhood is admitting when you are wrong.

Never, ever tell your girlfriend or wife that her new teeth braces look like the grill of your pick-up. Never!

When you're far away, aim high and remember the wind.

I believe you can tell a lot about the character of a man by his handshake, always extend your hand and grip firmly, it communicates confidence.

Remember, once you are over the hill, you pick up speed.

Don't squat with your spurs on.

Your cowboy boots will get a lot tougher to get on and off, the older you get.

Always be cautious of people who make promises you know they can't keep. This includes most politicians.

It's very difficult, if not impossible, to fill another man's boots. Be content with who you are and always be yourself.

Always be willing to lend a helping hand. And never be too proud to ask for one.

Be willing to work hard for the things you want. You will appreciate them that much more. A little prayer never hurts either.

Read the Bible a little bit every single day, you will be a better man for it.

Time spent on your knees in prayer is priceless.

Slaps in the face sting like heck, so don't say or do anything to a woman that might get you one.

Beautiful sunrises and sunsets are a lot more beautiful when you share them with someone you love.

It should be quite evident why God gave you two ears and only one mouth.

The biggest trouble maker in your life will be the guy who watches you shave and brush your teeth in the mirror every morning.

Never ask others for forgiveness until you can forgive others.

Sorrow and heartache is like carrying a big rock, the longer you carry it the heavier it gets.

Live a good, honorable life, and when you're my age and think back, you can enjoy it a second time.

Don't judge a book or a person by their cover. It's what's inside that counts.

Never be afraid to try.

Learn to say, "Thanks, Honey, that's just the way I like it", even when the yolks are hard and the biscuits burnt.

Impress people by the way you live your life, not by the things you can buy.

"Please" will get you a lot further down the road than "Give me".

Life is like a shadow on the ground, it changes by the second.

Your dog is the best example of a loyal friend that I can think of. You can tell it all your troubles, forget to feed it, leave it out in the weather, yell at it and call it names. It will always greet you with a wagging tail and loving lick. If you need proof, lock your wife or girlfriend in the trunk of your car along with your dog and see which one is happier to see you when you open it again.

Compliment people every chance you get, they like to hear it just as much as you.

You need clouds in your life before you can have silver linings.

The only people you need to get even with are the ones that helped you along the way.

There is nothing like the smell right after a rain or the sight of a rainbow. Stop whatever you're are doing and enjoy them. Then thank God for them.

Afternoon naps recharge your batteries, you'll need more recharging the older you get.

There is so much more to life than a series of 8 second rides with a shiny gold buckle waiting at the end. Life will buck you off more times than you can count, always pick yourself up, dust yourself off and get right back on again.

Don't ever expect life to be fair.

There are three kinds of people in this world. Those that make things happen, those that let things happen, and those poor souls that don't even have a suspicion. Try to be a leader, not a follower.

Don't ever smoke or chew or you'll burn holes in your favorite shirt or have slobber running down the side of your pick-up. Not cool!

Always be a gentleman and treat your gal with respect, open doors for her, and slide out her chairs. Give her a flower on special occasions. Yeah, your buddies will call you a wuss but your gal with think you're special.

Never raise your hand to a woman in anger.

Sins are sins, there's no such thing as big ones or little ones.

Be responsible, if you commit a crime; be prepared to do the time.

If you don't tell lies, you won't have to worry about remembering everything you said in the past.

Treat law enforcement officers with respect, they deserve it and besides, they have the unique ability to make your life miserable.

Thank God before eating his bounty at every meal.

Whenever you are introduced to a person, man or woman, extend your hand. It's a form of hospitality and welcome.

Use napkins to wipe your mouth, not to blow your nose, especially in the presence of women.

Alcohol on your breath hurts your credibility.

Drinking alcohol is not a right of passage and has absolutely no connection to manliness. Drink in moderation if you can handle it, and don't drink if you can't. It's that simple. Nothing good ever happens when you drink too much.

You can't be lost if you don't care where you are.

Once I opened a door for a liberated woman who immediately turned and asked me if I opened the door just because she was a woman? "No, ma'am", I said, "I opened the door for you just because I'm a gentleman, don't have a darn thing to do with what you are." Always try to be a gentleman, it's not that tough, and be proud of it. There's getting to be fewer and fewer of 'em.

As long as you are physically able, pray on your knees, it's a tangible way to show God respect.

If you don't know what it is, or what it does, don't mess with it.

When you are just about ready to "throw in the towel", remember that God never gives you more than you can handle. If God brings you to it, He will bring you through it.

Humility is a very worthy virtue and playing golf is the fastest way to learn it.

Too much alcohol always makes you think you're smarter than you really are.

Things can change, never tattoo a woman's name on your body, your horse's or dog's name is a better choice.

I know your grandma says that eating bacon and butter will kill you, and she just might be right. But I've been hearing that now for over 37 years, so it must be an awful slow death.

Someday when you have children of your own, they will break your rules, don't over react. Make the punishment fit the crime. I can't count the number of times I grounded your mother for life, never once thinking that I'd be gone long before her. So how would I ever know if she obeyed?

Always address your gal's folks as "sir" and "ma'am" unless invited to do otherwise.

Most any male can be a sperm donor, not near as many can be a good father.

Kids might not be planned but they are never mistakes. God never makes mistakes.

Only God knows if caterpillars and box turtles ever get where they're going.

Never carry your gun with a bullet in the chamber.

As long as grandma and I have been together, I have always helped her clear the table and do the dishes, do the same for your gal.

Respect and trust are not presents to be handed out, they both must be earned, and once either is lost, they are hard to get back, if ever.

By and large, Democrats are good people who pretty much want the same things you do; they just go about gettin' it the wrong way.

Liberals are really just very angry Democrats. Their ideas will always cost you freedoms or money. Avoid them like you would an angry skunk.

Always wear your jeans up around your waist and wear your ball cap with the bill facing forward. At least people will think you know if you're coming or going, even if you really don't.

Learn to cook and how to wash clothes, there might not always be someone around to do it for you.

Yes, ducks, geese, and cranes do get tired from flying all day. That's why they stop to rest all night.

Sometimes a simple roll of toilet paper can be a prized possession. Always know where to get one in a hurry and remember what I said about squatting with your spurs on.

It's okay to be scared or afraid, they make you cautious.

Bluebirds, orioles, and yellow finches are living proof that God thought of everything.

An old friend told me once that only pirates pierce their ears, so if you ever come home with pierced ears, there better be a ship out in the front yard.

Your dad, your grandpas and someday your sons and grandsons are the only men you should ever kiss, ever.

Tell people that you love them often, there will come a day when you wish you could.

When you close your eyes and think of simple pleasures, Oreo cookies soaked in ice cold milk will always make the cut.

Fish fight 'cause they don't want to get in the boat, really.

If you want to put a smile on a young ladies' face, kiss the back of her hand.

Call your banker by his first name, greet him with a handshake and always ask about his family. It will make your business with him a lot easier.

I know your mom and your grandma think they know most everything. No harm, just let 'em keep on thinkin' it.

I used to tell my friends that if there was ever anything they couldn't figure out on their own, to call your mom, 'cause she had all the answers. That really made her angry and I think hurt a little, I should have known better.

Thank God that your mom and grandma don't charge a fee for their advice. The bill would resemble the national debt.

Never go to bed angry.

I learned years ago that there is a direct relationship between big mouths and small brains.

It's hard to respect others without first respecting yourself.

Everybody, and I mean everybody, sins, makes mistakes, and errors in judgment, so don't get down on yourself if you do. There was only one perfect being, His name was Jesus Christ.

There is a big difference between "self-esteem" and "self-respect". Self-esteem is liking yourself for what you can do; self-respect is liking yourself for who you are. Learn to tell the difference, and if you have to choose between the two, take self-respect.

If you absolutely have to pick your nose or your seat, do it in private.

Live simply, try to avoid borrowing money, but if you must, don't borrow more than you can comfortably pay back and pay it back as quickly as you can.

It's far better to be a good listener than a talking head.

I often ask others for their perspective about subjects that trouble me. If you do, respect their opinion, especially since you asked for it; but keep in mind that opinions are like noses and butts, most everybody will have one.

Try your best to be a good listener, look people directly in the eyes when they speak and don't interrupt.

Until you are lucky enough to be your own boss, do what your boss tells you, even when you don't agree.

It is always more comforting when someone else wipes away your tears of sorrow.

You can have many loves in your lifetime, but only one mom. Never lose sight of that, and always treat her like someone very special, 'cause she is.

Always mend fences with your friends and neighbors even if you weren't the one who cut 'em.

You can only reap what you sow. Sow good things like love, patience, understanding, forgiveness, humility and your harvest will always be bountiful.

You can always learn a lot from watching livestock and wildlife. Learn to trust your instincts. If it looks like a duck, swims like a duck, quacks like a duck; chances are pretty darn good that it's a duck.

Try not to stare at a woman's body parts, but for those times when you just can't help yourself, be wearing your sun glasses.

There's a real knack to knowing which cow pies you can kick and which ones you can't, until you learn it, it's best to just step over 'em or go around 'em, especially on a hot day.

The wind usually blows out here so always head into the wind when you're stalking game, and never spit into it.

There are some people who will never hear a Bobwhite whistle, a coyote howl, or see an eagle soar, that's a shame.

Republicans are not always right, and Democrats not always wrong, just mostly.

Think twice before wearing a bow tie with a cowboy shirt.

If you're riding on a high horse, there's no way to get down gracefully.

Never wipe your nose or your mouth in the sleeve of your shirt unless it's an emergency, and never at the supper table, no matter what.

The art of riding a horse is keeping the horse between you and the ground.

Girls seem to like a man who can dance, if you want to meet a lot of young ladies, learn to dance. You don't have to like it, just do it.

If you don't know where you're goin', it's probably a good idea not to use your spurs.

Several of my friends say that I look like a wounded Rhinoceros when I dance, but, I wonder how many of them have ever seen a wounded Rhino two step?

You don't have to kneel and pray every time you want to talk to God. It's really no different than talking to me or your dad. God is always there and always listening.

A cowboy is one who says that it was nothin' when it was everything.

Always keep a healthy supply of dog treats in your pick-up. It will make the journey to your neighbor's front door a lot easier.

Never leave home without your pocket cross and rub it often to remind yourself that God loves you.

When you lose, don't lose the lesson.

You weren't born with your hat on your head so know when to remove it, and don't worry; you are not the only person to get hat hair.

Have heard it said that the only good reason to ride a bull is to meet a pretty nurse.

Always get the manure off your boots and remove your hat went entering the Lord's house.

It's okay to stop and ask for directions, and especially well advised on the long journey of life.

In matters of love, never ask a question of a gal when the answer might break your heart unless you're prepared to deal with a broken heart.

Don't be afraid to go after what you want, or what you want to be. But always be willing to pay the price.

Be humble when saying you're sorry or asking for forgiveness. Holding your hat in your hand is a good start.

Never judge your gal by her relatives.

No one says "it's only a game" when their team is winning.

Pray for things that matter, God doesn't really care what you drive, so don't waste His time and yours praying for a new pick-up.

Bad things do happen to good people.

Always be yourself because the people that matter don't mind . . . and the ones that mind don't matter.

Life isn't tied with a bow . . . but it's still a gift.

Every new day is created by God, thank Him for it.

If you always help your neighbors brand their calves, you'll never be short handed when it's time to brand your own.

When choosing your life's work, keep in mind that not everybody would make a good doctor or lawyer, but not everybody would make a good ranch hand either.

There is no shame in working with your hands and your back for a living. Do your work heartily; it's the Lord for whom you really work.

A callused hand is usually a strong hand.

Bunions hurt like the devil, always wear boots that fit.

Few things are more relaxing than flying a kite or skipping rocks. Do them every chance you get, especially with your kids.

Once a long time ago, while having a little disagreement with your grandma, I told her that I'd like to agree with her, but if I did, then we'd both be wrong. I've never said it since. It's okay to think it, just don't ever say it.

Sometimes during your life you will lose your perspective, women seem to have a real talent for getting it back for you.

If you read the Bible and worship regularly, you will hear the words "mercy" and "grace" often. Think about them like this. "Mercy" is not getting punished even though you deserve to. "Grace" is getting something nice even though you don't deserve to.

Always try and sleep where you can see the stars, somehow they magically help you forget the troubles of the day.

Sometimes I wish the little voice inside me would just be silent.

Some people say that there are no do-overs in real life, they're mistaken, for Christians every new day is a mulligan.

Big cities are a good place to go a few times a year to visit friends or stock up on supplies. They're not a good place to spend your life or raise your kids.

I guess I don't really know and surely couldn't explain why my eyes well up with tears when I hear the Star Spangled Banner; but I'm not ashamed of it.

Whenever a funeral procession crosses your path, lower your head and ask the Lord to comfort the family and loved ones left behind. It's too late to pray for the person in the coffin.

Whenever you're in grandma's presence, cheer for the Green Bay Packers, and never, ever switch channels when she's watchin' them on TV.

The two most beautiful prayers ever sung are *God Bless America* and *The Lord's Prayer.*

I don't know why Mourning Doves sound so sad and lonely, but they sure do.

Love is not a game; there are no winners or losers, just joys and sorrows.

Cursing and swearing is a bad habit to get into although I think most people have done it a time or two. Even grandma does it now and then, except she tries to do it under her breath so no one hears.

Never spend hard earned money for a cat. I'm sure God had more in mind for 'em than catching mice. I just don't know what that would be though.

A long line of smoke on the horizon usually means a prairie fire. Always grab a shovel and head that way. Those fighting the fire can always use an extra hand.

The saddest sounds I've ever heard are *Taps* blown by a distant bugler and a piper playing *Amazing Grace* on a bagpipe; they always send chills up my spine and put a lump in my throat.

People out here just take stars for granted; there are people who live in big cities that never see them, if they only knew what they were missing.

As many times as sheep and shepherds are referenced in the Bible, I've never understood why they always seem to get such a bad rap.

Always, always make your first jump into a strange lake feet first.

I have heard it said that silence is golden, don't know about that, but do know it's darn valuable.

All you can do is all you can do, just don't ever quit.

Turn to the Lord often out of gratitude and you won't be a stranger when you turn to him in desperation; and you will.

If you're the first one on the serving bowl, always leave enough to make it around the table at least once. And when there's only one portion left, ask if anyone wants to share.

Try and make your home where the seasons change, each season has its very own beauty. Just visit all those other places.

Plant lots of trees, their splendor as they change with the seasons will take your breath away.

You will probably live a lot longer than grandpa so take good care of your body. I wish I would have. They make replacement parts, and I have a few, but they never seem to work as well as your original equipment and they are darn expensive.

Set a goal for yourself that when the Lord calls you home, you leave no man or woman behind that is glad to see you go, I still have some work to do.

When a cook serves something you're not too fond of, never snub your nose. Take a small helping, leave it on your plate and claim you are too full to eat it. Men cooks won't care if you snub your nose, but some women cooks take it real personal.

If you think you want to be a rodeo cowboy, your mom and grandma would like you to take a long look at calf roping. Leave the bucking events to cowboys who don't think they will ever get old and have a lot of money for those replacement parts.

Remember you are never as tough as you think you are, or want to be.

Ask God early for a goodly share of patience, you'll need plenty.

When you are having words with a woman, more times than not, you won't get to use yours.

When you are my age, as hard as it might be to get down on the floor to play with your grandkids, do it anyway. The laughter and joy on their faces will reward your effort, and somebody will always help you get back up.

Being able to poke fun at yourself is a sure sign of self-confidence. It takes a good man not to poke fun at others.

While your children and grandkids are small, help them plant a tree the same size as they are and watch them grow together. Someday when you're gone, they will look at that tree and think of you.

I've heard it said that cowboys who ride bulls were probably not their class valedictorian.

Buy a camera and keep it close. Take lots of pictures of friends, loved ones, beautiful things and places, if you do, you won't have to try near as hard to remember the things you wish you could when you are my age.

God loves us far too much to make bad things happen, but he allows bad things to happen to teach us and do his will.

There's a big, big difference between growing older and growing up. Growing older is mandatory, growing up is optional.

Our Lord doesn't make deals, so don't waste your time by including "If You" closely followed by "I will" in any of your prayers or conversations with Him.

Never think of a cat as a pet. Keep a few around the place to keep rodents away, treat 'em as you would any of God's creatures, but never let 'em indoors. Think of 'em as a four legged hired hand.

I used to find it amusing how many men wore cowboy hats that probably never even walked past a horse, then grandma pointed out that most likely, a very large number of men who wear baseball caps never played baseball either. She's a smart woman.

God only promises a safe landing, not a calm passage.

Always seek good counsel when about to make an important decision. There's no better place to start than on your knees.

There was a period of time in my life that I thought I was really big and important. Then once while on vacation, I stood on the rim of the Grand Canyon, and it didn't take very long for me to realize how infinitesimal I really am.

Politely listen to advice given to you by others but always listen closest to the voice inside yourself.

I've heard it said that you can tell a lot about a man by the kind of pet he owns. When you decide to get a dog, give Labradors strong consideration. I've always found them to be big, strong, mostly silent, very loyal, obedient, easy going, gentle, good with kids, and great hunters and swimmers, heck, they are most everything I want to be.

It's true that a person can never have too many friends, and good friends are like angels, you don't have to see them to know they are there.

A good hunt is not measured by what's in your game bag or the size of the rack. Enjoy the sights, smells, sounds of creation, and the time spent with buddies. On some of my most memorable hunts, I never fired a single shot.

People my age usually don't have regrets for what we did, but rather for what we didn't do, and I have some.

Don't over-harvest the fish or game. Take what you need for a meal or two, thank God for the experience and leave the rest to help you create new memories.

Exercise your right to vote every time you're given the opportunity. Thousands of good men and women gave their lives so you have that right. Don't let their memories and sacrifices be in vain.

If you are ever wondering how you should vote, get your Bible and read Ecclesiastes 10:2. That verse should help you decide.

Always respect the American Flag and those brave men and women who defend it every day. If your country ever calls on you to defend it, do it with determination and honor.

Let your faith always be greater than your fear.

When your mother was young, every morning before sending her off to school I'd kiss the palm of her hand and tell her that if she ever needed a hug during the day to hold that palm up next to her cheek to remind her how much I loved her. Do the same, not just for your kids but all those you love. Often times I lay in bed at night regretting that I didn't kiss more palms. I find a lot of comfort in believing that the last thing God does before sending every new baby out into the world is kiss their palm.

Go out of your way to thank and show appreciation for any veteran or person still wearing the uniform of their country. And if you can, pick up their tab.

I have always been in awe of thunderstorms, and spend a lot time on stormy nights just sitting in the dark watching and listening. I believe thunder is the Lord's way of telling me, "We need to talk", and we do.

You will have to go to school when you are a young lad growing up; it's the law, so make the best of it. Pay attention and study hard, when you are my age you will be glad you did, although try as I might, I can never remember using algebra.

I believe that athletics not only make you a better student but also teach you skills that you can use your entire life. Not everybody can be the starting quarterback or pitcher, that's why they are called "team" sports. And I'd bet your gal will still think you are special even if you sit the pines.

Life is not a race that you run, but a long journey that you take, and it's mostly up hill and often into a head wind.

There is a huge difference between being a good sport and a good loser. A good sport is gracious and humble in both victory and defeat. A good loser is still a loser.

Laugh, laugh, and laugh even more. Laugh often, long and hard. Try to make others laugh too. Tears from laughter are much sweeter than tears from sorrow. Never laugh at others, only with them, and don't be afraid to laugh at yourself.

Don't be in a hurry to grow up. Play cowboys and Indians, cops and robbers, crawl on your hands and knees driving your toy trucks. You will grow up soon enough. Grandma still tells me to grow up from time to time, but I don't think I ever really want to, at least all the way.

Sing, make joyous noise every chance you get. Sing in church, in the shower, runnin' on down the highway in your pick-up and while you're working. Sing to your kids and even your gal or wife. Singing will keep your heart young. And many songs have a way of saying things that you think but can't put into words. Music is what feelings sound like.

They say "Absence makes the heart grow fonder", but I think absence with a broken heart only makes the heart grow heavier. And time does not heal all wounds, some wounds never heal, all you do is pick up the pieces and carry on as best you can.

When you are praying or just talking with the Lord, don't worry about finding the right words, He already knows what you want to say.

One of the hardest decisions you'll ever face in life is choosing whether to walk away, or try harder.

During your life you will probably have many romances, and you will believe that each one is "the" one, but more than likely, your heart will be broken a time or two. Reminisce and learn from each broken heart because they will help mold you into the man that some young lady will think is truly "the" one.

When you are down to your last round of ammunition, relax, take a deep breath, take careful aim and make it count.

Always be on the lookout for people who might be down on their luck and need a helping hand. Be willing to offer that helping hand any way you can, money, food, clothes, whatever it takes, 'cause everything you have was given to you as a blessing, everything!

Don't ever let the collection plate pass by you without giving the Lord His due. And don't think of your offering as just another bill that must be paid, it is a form of worship.

You will find that not all people share your beliefs, especially when it comes to faith and how you worship the Lord. It is important to respect the beliefs of others whether or not you agree with them.

We Christians observe Christmas and Easter, Jews observe Passover and Hanukah. Atheists observe April Fool's Day, and rightly so.

Some dates are real important to remember, loved one's birthdays rank up there pretty high. And unless you really enjoy sleepin' in your pick-up, don't ever forget your wedding anniversary.

Your gal or wife should never have to cook on three occasions, her birthday, Mother's Day, and your anniversary. On those special days, take her out to a nice restaurant instead, and a bottle of wine or flowers is also a nice touch.

"Pity" is an ugly word that implies you are better than another person. You can have compassion or sympathy for another, but never pity them. And as long as you know how to pray, you'll never have cause to pity yourself.

You make a living by what you get; you make a life by what you give.

There is a very fine line between pride and conceit, be careful not to cross it. Conceit changes a man, you might like what you see in the mirror but your friends won't like what they see when looking at you.

Sometimes it dawns on me that I don't understand everything I know.

Attend to your own business and let others mind theirs, don't gossip or listen to those who do. If you are not willing to say it to another's face, it's best not to say it, period.

Read a lot of good books. History books will teach you about your birthright, documentaries will enlighten you, political books will sometimes make you angry and the Bible will give you peace. Your mind will always stay sharp if you read.

Time can be so cruel, when you're in a hospital waiting room yearning for news, and you want it to fly, it passes oh so slowly: but when you're in the arms of your lover and never want the moment to end, it flies

"Bucket List" is a catchy term for a list of things you want to do before you die. You will have a lot of years to make your list. I have two bucket lists, one I can share with people, the other I can't. And for those old folks who don't have a bucket list, I can't help but wonder what motivates them to get out of bed every morning.

You'll often hear people my age say, "I don't know what I'd do with myself if I retired." Feel sorry for them.

If your girlfriend or wife ever tells you she wants to be treated like one of the guys, it might be a good indication that you're spending too much time with the guys.

I like to be on a first name basis with my physician, I would have difficulty allowing a stranger to do to me what he has to do.

I also like to call my pastor by his first name when we are out of the sanctuary. I'm sure several of my Christian friends find that irreverent, but it sure makes it easier for me to tell him what's troubling me.

Family traditions are a nice way of remembering those we love, those still with us and those who aren't. Your great grandma's sugar cookies at Christmas time is one tradition you should always keep.

The most beautiful and powerful hymn I've ever heard is "How Great Thou Art". When you hear it, close your eyes and just concentrate on the words.

I've wasted a lot of time looking, but have yet to find a suitable substitute for plain old common sense.

One of your grandma's sisters had a little retort when people would razz her a little. She'd ask," Was that kind, necessary and true?" Ask yourself that when what you are about to say might sting someone. And just for the record, that sister seldom practiced what she preached.

Golf is game I love to hate. I always swing at the ball real hard just in case I hit it. Your best round is just a few strokes shy of being your worst. And if you golf, don't confuse luck with skill.

Unless you're a slacker, never be afraid to ask others how they think you're doin'. But also be prepared for how they might answer.

Experience is a wonderful teacher, but the lessons are not always pleasant.

Independence can be very rewarding and satisfying, and very lonely too.

Getting old is a lot more fun than being old but a friend once told me that it's still the best alternative.

Guess I never fully understood what it meant to be "comfortable in my own skin". I always figured I was, but then again, I didn't know I had a choice. Don't talk in riddles.

Your mother was very independent when she was growing up; she stretched her wings and wanted to fly solo earlier than most. I don't think she ever anticipated all the crash landings though. She still carries a few scars as reminders. It's good to look at old scars and remember how we got them.

Real courage is knowing that what you are about to attempt is next to impossible, and you continue on anyway.

Life is too short, ride your best horse first.

Your mom often reminded me of an old shop radio I had, it was either blaring or giving me static and was harder than the dickens to get tuned in.

I was pretty strict with your mom, I was one of those "my way or the highway" dads. Don't be like I was. God, how I wish I could go back in time and raise her again.

When I go home, don't dwell on my death but rather my life and take all that love you have for me and spread it around.

Just because the trail you're followin' is well marked, doesn't mean the person who marked it knew where they were headed.

If you ever have the opportunity to speak in front of a group of people, shy away from using the word "I" very often.

If you don't know something, just own up, it's okay. But then turn around and try to learn what you didn't know.

Don't beat around the bush, always say what you mean and, more importantly, mean what you say.

It's fun to go out and have a few with the guys now and then, but know when to call it a night. You'll never soar with the eagles all day when you've been out hootin' with the owls all night.

Unfortunately, not only stupid people do stupid things, stupidity is an equal opportunity affliction.

It is true, what goes around usually comes around, and in most cases, it's going a lot faster.

I've found that the easiest way to eat crow is while it's still warm. The colder it gets, the harder it is to swallow.

For me, working out is like hitting my thumb with a hammer, it always feels so dang good when I stop. I'll never have those 6 pack abs and I've known that for over half a century. I'm okay with it.

Never could understand why some people think it's silly to wear both suspenders and a belt at the same time, you back up your computer don't you?

When you close your eyes and imagine "freedom" what comes to mind? Most people would say noble things like freedom of religion, the Bill of Rights, or the Constitution. For me it's always been the wind, nothing is as free as the wind; you never know where it came from, or where it's going.

Probably the one question you will ask most in your life, and the hardest one to get answered, at least with an answer you can accept and live with, is "why?" Sometimes, only God knows the answer.

You can never control what others do to you or say about you, but you can always control how you react.

Remember, it's not enough to learn how to ride; you also have to learn how to fall.

Good judgment comes from experience and a lotta' that comes from bad judgment.

The way you are seen by other people directly reflects on your upbringing. Never give people reason to believe you were found lying on the prairie and raised by a pack of coyotes.

Think of life as a never ending lesson, some lessons you learn easily and others the hard way. Early on I set a goal to try and learn at least one new thing every day, doesn't have to be earth shaking. Why, when, where and how are words I used often.

Live each day as though it is your last, and treat all your friends and loved ones as if it were theirs. Someday, it will be. This is a lot easier said than done, and some days I failed miserably.

When it comes to atheists, thank God they are wrong.

Tellin' someone to get lost and makin' 'em do it are two different propositions.

Try and never lose track of the people you love and care about, you may never be able to find them again and their absence leaves an awful hole in your heart.

There is nothing you could ever do, no sin big enough, to disqualify you from God's grace.

Son,

I know I've given you an awful lot of things to think about, chances are you won't remember them all, and that's okay. But the one thing I hope you never forget is how much your grandpa loves you. I have thought for many years that I was the most generously blessed man on earth, and when God blessed me with you, I was convinced. When the Lord takes me home, be strong for your grandma and every night when you go to bed, think of you and me, the fun times we had together, and smile. I'll always be up ahead, on down the road a piece waitin' for you to catch up.

Love,
Papa

THINGS I WANTED MY GRANDSONS TO KNOW

before I leave

CHAPTER 2

Written by a loving grandfather for his two grandsons, *Things I Wanted My Grandsons to Know Before I Leave* presents a collection of quotes, sayings, snippets, and observations that author Kenn Stobbe believes helped him to live a successful, God-centered life

Kenn's grandsons were born to his only child, an adopted daughter. The boys became the sons the older man never had, both were born when he was already in his sixties. Today, a combination of school, distance, sporting events limits his one on one time to share those things that comprised his moral compass with the boys. Now in his 70's and the winter of his life, Kenn—thinking he would not live long enough to pass any words of wisdom along to his grandsons as they were growing up—decided to write them out instead.

His primary objective is to help his grandsons live the same type of life he has himself. As part of this collection, Kenn addresses, life, love, common sense, manners, morals, values, and beliefs, with a sprinkling of his own thoughts and opinions. Some of the entries are humorous, while others are more serious and thought-provoking.

Things I Wanted My Grandsons to Know Before I Leave offers a heartwarming glimpse into the character and integrity of one man and into the depth of his love for his grandsons.

KENN STOBBE has always admired the cowboy way of life-simple, hardowkring, and honest. He and his wife, Jan, make their home in ranching country northwest of Burwell, Nebraska, in the beautiful Nebraska Sandhills

kennstobbe.com.

*To my wife and best buddy, Jan
who was willing to take a chance
on me 43 years ago*

Introduction

My dearest Grayson and Talon,

"Papa" was already an old man when you two were born so chances of me being around to share these things while you are growing up are not very promising. When I was in highschool, I became entertained by reading old sayings, and quotations and tried to remember and apply them to my own life as situations arose. Soon my interest blossomed into a hobby and I had to start writing them down rather than forget them. Some I read, others were told to me by friends and loved ones. and still others were my own thoughts. Many made me laugh, and many brought tears to my eyes, but all made me think. I thought all were worth knowing and remembering. As the years passed, the list grew and grew and I believe my library of old sayings, quotations, snippets, lessons, beliefs, and observations helped make me who I am today. You two are the sons I never had and my intent is to share them with you now in hopes they might make you a better person, and your journey through this life just a little easier. Only you, your loved ones and friends will ever know if I accomplished my goal.

Always remember, there is a God, one God, and his love for you is unconditional and never ending.

Backin' down ain't always the opposite of backin' up. And when it's not, it often requires humility and courage.

You can't weigh the facts if the scales are weighed down with your own opinions.

Sometimes worry can give a small thing a big shadow.

Knowin' what you don't know is the beginnin' of wisdom.

If you want to liven up the conversation, just say the right thing, the wrong way.

Some men talk 'cause they got somethin' to say. Others talk 'cause they got to say somethin'.

Life will give you thousands of opportunities to keep your mouth shut.

To avoid the mistakes of youth, draw from the wisdom of age.

Nothin' keeps you honest more than witnesses.

The reason windshields are so big, and rear view mirrors so small is because it's a lot more important to know where you're goin' than where you've been.

You're not bein' diplomatic just 'cause you put "please" in front of "Shut the hell up."

The quieter you are, the more you can hear.

Anything is possible if you don't know what you're talkin' about.

Trouble is a private thing, don't lend it and don't borrow it.

If you always do what you have done, you will always get what you have got.

The true measure of success depends on who's doin' the measurein'.

Don't try and open your button fly jeans with your gloves on, especially if you're in a hurry.

Determination is knowin' that you're gettin' bucked off before you ever get on, but saddlin' up anyway.

Words that soak into your ears are whispered, not yelled.

It don't take a very big man to carry a grudge.

Being neighborly don't mean stickin' your nose in somebody's business.

It is easier to patch a broken mirror than a reputation.

You can't solve problems by using the same kind of thinkin' you used to create 'em.

God made you a male, but makin' yourself a man is up to you.

There's an old sayin', "He who dies with the most toys, wins", but come to think of it, I've never seen a hearse towin' a U-Haul.

Some fellas have more wishbone than backbone.

Never worry about tomorrow, God is already there.

Time heals 'most everything, but you have to give time time.

Be the type of man that leaves a mark, not a scar.

When trust is broken, sorry means nothing.

A shallow stream is noisiest.

I hope you never hate any man enough to pray for his passin', however, I find it perfectly acceptable to find some pleasure in readin' his obituary.

It's tough sometimes, but try and remember that life is 10% what happens to you and 90% how you react to it.

If you take the time it takes, it takes less time.

There is nothing like facts to mess up a good story.

There's a big difference between "wants" and "needs". Believe in the Lord and He promises to give you all your needs, but not necessarily all your wants. You'd be wise to learn that early on, I wish I had.

Forgettin' and laughin' is much better than rememberin' and cryin'.

Great minds talk about ideas, average minds talk about events, small minds talk about people.

Life ain't always fair, sometimes you're the windshield, and sometimes you're the bug.

When I first started wearin' hearin' aids, I thought they were a curse. Then one day I discovered an on/off switch and they became a blessin' in disguise; now I don't always hear all of grandma's "instructions" and free advice.

If you find something you really want, go after it. Yea, waitin' can be hard, but not as hard as regrettin'.

Never buy a dog when you've had too much to drink.

Every breath you take, every beat of your heart is a gift, a blessing from God.

Never apologize for how you feel, it's like saying sorry for being real.

Some things are better left unsaid, and you'll probably realize that right after you've just said 'em.

Don't corner a critter that you know is meaner than you.

You'll never get a second chance to make a first impression.

"Time heals all wounds." Not true, the truth is that the passage of time only dulls the ache, nothing takes the pain away completely.

Sometimes not gettin' what you want is a stroke of luck.

Ducks flyin' overhead in the woods are generally headed towards water.

Even a blind squirrel finds an acorn every now and then.

"Conscience" is not only hard to spell, but harder to explain. You can't see or touch it, it's a feelin' in your heart or thought in your mind that guides you to do right. My father told me never to do anything durin' the day that would keep me awake durin' the night. Lookin' back on my life, I wish I would have listened more closely to his advice.

Some of the most valuable lessons in life can be learned from a hungry stomach, an empty wallet and a broken heart.

Kindness doesn't cost a thing, but it's the richest gift you can give.

Most of the stuff people worry about in life never happens.

Sometimes tryin' to forget someone you once loved is like tryin' to put toothpaste back in the tube.

There are two theories about arguin' with a woman, and neither one works.

If your girl or your wife ever says "Correct me if I'm wrong." Don't, under any circumstance, utter so much as a word! Never!

Knowin' God's laws is the easy part of bein' a Christian, keepin' 'em is the hard part.

An old timer is a man who's had a lot of interestin' experiences – and some of 'em are even true.

As you grow older, especially if you are a Christian, you will often hear the word "faith". Faith is the confidence that what we hope for will actually happen; it gives us assurance about things we cannot see.

Just because you're strugglin', don't mean you're failin'.

Once you lie, everything you say after that loses credibility.

"You'll never reach your destination if you stop and throw rocks at every dog that barks" (Winston Churchill)

The only thing you get from straddlin' the fence on an issue is a sore crotch.

Always make prayer a first priority, instead of a last resort.

Don't mess with somethin' that ain't botherin' you none.

Sometimes you get and sometimes you get got.

If you focus on the hurt, you will continue to suffer. But if you focus on the lesson, you will continue to grow.

To trust God in the light is nothin', but to trust Him in the dark, now that's faith.

Never chase love, affection, or attention, if it isn't given freely by another person, it ain't worth havin'.

Worryin' is like puttin' up your umbrella before it rains, It ain't no use.

You can't unsay a cruel thing.

Always give thanks for the small blessings in life, sometimes we never really appreciate them until they're gone; toilet paper is a good example.

Few things smell better then fresh cut alfalfa just after a rain.

Live simply. Love generously. Care deeply. Speak kindly, and leave the rest to God.

Havin' somewhere to go is home, havin' someone to love is family, havin' both is a blessin'.

Liberals think we should all be equal at the finish line, conservatives think we should all be equal at the startin' line.

God's grace is like a gentle voice that says. "Here is the world. Terrible and beautiful things will happen to you. But don't be afraid. I am with you."

God does not forgive excuses, only sin.

Every path has some puddles.

Never drive black cattle in the dark.

Never make your girlfriend or wife angry, 'cause they can remember things that haven't even happened yet.

Every morning when you wake up, go outside and take a look around at what God has created. Creation is the signpost pointin' to the majesty of God.

Remember, real cowboys don't line dance.

Sometime the memory is worse than the actual event.

If you can't sing -- dance.

Think long and hard before acceptin' another man's wager, he wouldn't make the offer if he didn't know somethin' you don't.

No matter how many times a snake sheds its skin, it will always be a snake. Remember that before allowin' certain people back in your life.

Never ruin an apology with an excuse.

Prayer is a powerful gift from God, do it often in both good times and in bad. He has promised to hear you, that He will answer you, and that his answer will always be for your good.

Always ride your horse in the direction it's goin'.

It's a whole lot more enjoyable fallin' in love than it is fallin' out.

A secret is usually somethin' that's told to many people, but only one at a time.

If you can't take the time to do things right the first time, where are ya' gonna find the time to do it the second time?

Logic does not always convince the heart.

You can never tell which direction a frog will jump by the size of its feet.

A goal without plan is just a wish.

Always sing like nobody's listenin' and dance like nobody's watchin'.

You are loved when you are born and you'll be loved when you die. In between, you just have to manage!

In life, it's important to know when to stop arguing with people and just let them be wrong.

Never ask a man the size of his spread.

When you make a promise you build hope. When you keep it you build trust.

After eatin' an entire bull, a mountain lion felt so good he started roarin'. He kept it up until a hunter came along and shot him.... The moral: When you're full of bull, keep yer mouth shut.

"Avoiding a fight is a mark of honor;......" (Proverbs 20:3). A man confident of his strength doesn't need to parade it, and a brave man doesn't look for chances to prove it.

Life always offers you a second chance. It's called tomorrow.

One simple fact of life you should always try to remember is that a woman has the last word in any disagreement. Anythin' you say after that is the beginnin' of a new disagreement.

Courage is what it takes to stand up and speak. Courage is also what it takes to sit down and listen. (Winston Churchill)

A good horse never comes in a bad color.

Kenn Stobbe

Sometimes it is wise to seek the advice of others, if you do, always remember you'll probably only take their advice if it agrees with the decision you've already made or is an easier path to take. It's human nature to reject help and do things our way.

If a woman begins a conversation with "First of all'", you are in trouble.

Always mean what you say, just don't always say it out loud.

What you appear to be isn't nearly as important as what you are.

Never trust your dog to watch your food.

God gave us all something to fall back on, and sooner or later we'll all land flat on it.

Always be an optimist, at least until they start movin' animals in pairs to Cape Canaveral.

I believe patience has its limits. Take it too far, and it's cowardice.

It took me far too many years to realize that a lot of people pray to receive those things that I take for granted.

Diplomacy is the art of sayin' "Nice doggie" until you can find a rock.

The challenge is not always sayin' what you mean, but to say it with as few words as possible.

Scars are just tattoos with better stories.

Winnin' ain't everything but losin' ain't fun either. Ride to win!!

I believe there are more tears shed over answered prayers than over unanswered prayers.

Never give up on somethin' you want, sure, waitin' is difficult, but it's even more difficult to regret.

Common sense is a flower that doesn't grow in everybody's garden.

Always grab what you can and let the loose ends drag.

Remember if it ain't dirty, it probably ain't fun.

If you want to be a cowboy when you grow up...you'll have to choose.

It doesn't matter how hard you hope and pray, sometimes you have to accept the fact that certain things will never go back to how they used to be.

"Fear is a reaction, courage is a decision" (Winston Churchill)

I am beginnin' to wonder if I'll ever be old enough to know better; I think your grandma is getting' a little concerned too.

There is a huge difference between "knowledge" (havin' the facts) and "wisdom" (applyin' those facts to life). You can accumulate knowledge, but without wisdom, your knowledge is useless. You must learn how to live out what you know. Knowing God is the key to wisdom.

Not everyone is meant to be in your future. Some people are just passin' through to teach you lessons in life.

It's better to cross the line and suffer the consequences than to just stare at the line for the rest of your life.

Female intuition is a 6th sense that all women have. Your grandma's is so highly developed; she sometimes knows I'm wrong before I've even opened my mouth.

Never hold a person to anything he says while he's drinkin', or runnin' for office.

If you don't do wild things while you're young, you'll have nothin' to shake your head and smile about when you're my age.

A beautiful sign that winter is not far off is the sight and sound of the Sandhill cranes headin' South. Stop whatever you're doin' and enjoy the moment.

Democracy is bein' allowed to vote for the candidate you dislike least.

You just can't beat the person who never gives up. (Babe Ruth)

I think it's better to be hated for who you are then loved for who you are not.

The United States can't eliminate income inequality until it eliminates effort inequality.

The nicest place to be is in someone's thoughts, the safest place to be is in someone's prayers,

Don't worry that no one knows of you; seek to be worth knowin'.

If you haven't grown up by the age of 50, forget it, chances are you never will.

Good times become good memories and bad times become good lessons.

There comes a time when you have to choose between turnin' the page or closin' the book.

You will come to know that what appears today to be a sacrifice will prove instead to be the greatest investment that you'll ever make.

While you're tryin' to teach your children all about life, your children will be teachin' you what life is all about.

There's a lot of pleasure in doin' somethin' people say you can't.

Good friends are hard to find, harder to leave, and impossible to forget.

Liberals are very broadminded: they're always willin' to give careful consideration to both sides of the same side.

Life is all about choices – and their consequences. As author Robert Lewis Stevenson once said, " Sooner or later everyone sits down to a banquet of consequences". When you make the right choices, you will have less reason to fear the consequences. Always ask the Lord for guidance when you have to make an important choice.

If you never try, you'll never know.

You know that little thing inside your head that keeps you from sayin' things you shouldn't? Grandma told me that mine quit workin' years ago.

Success is gettin' what you want, happiness is wantin' what you get.

You usually come to a conclusion when you get tired of thinkin'.

When you are my age, I hope you can look back at your life and say, "I can't believe I did that" instead of saying "I wish I did that".

Truth fears no questions.

Some people get angry because God put thorns on roses, while others praise him for putting roses among thorns.

As tough as it might be, at some point you have to realize that some people can stay in your heart, but not in your life.

Temper gets you into trouble. Pride keeps you there.

Judgin' a person does not define who they are, it defines who you are.

Be careful, when some people ask you for advice, what they're really lookin' for is an accomplice.

Someday is not a day of the week.

There is a big difference between a human bein' and bein' human, unfortunately only a few people understand that.

Even crime wouldn't pay if the government ran it.

Experience is a hard teacher. It gives the test first and the lessons afterwards.

A person who aims at nothin' is sure to hit it.

Contentment is not the fulfillment of what you want, but the realization of how much you already have.

Its amazin' how fast you can get a cowboy boot off if you stick your foot in and find some little critter has put it on before you.

One virtue I always wished I had a liitle more of is self-control. It's perfectly natural to feel anger from time to time, but you don't have to show it.

Experience is what causes a person to make new mistakes instead of old ones.

They say "Money talks"...but all I can remember mine sayin' was "good-bye".

Never argue with a fool. Someone watchin' may not be able to tell the difference.

Opportunity may knock only once, but temptation leans on the doorbell.

To make any marriage run smoothly: Practice saying," You know, dear, you may be right."

Even God can't change the past.

A liberal is a person whose interests ain't at stake at the moment.

Good friends are people who know you well, but like you anyway.

Hindsight is an exact science.

Most times, it just gets down to common sense.

I have often regretted my speech, but never my silence.

Success in marriage is not so much findin' the right person as it is bein' the right person.

Make it a practice to always read the fine print when something is advertised for "free". You won't find any fine print in the Word of God.

To be a winner, all you need to give is all you got.

You are only young once, but you can stay immature indefinitely.

One nice thing about egotists is they don't talk about other people.

It's true God won't give you anything you can't handle. But sometimes you'll wish he didn't trust you so much.

Never blame anyone in your life. The good people give you happiness, the bad give you experience, the worst give you a lesson and the best give you memories.

It's true that you only live once, but if you do it right, once is enough.

Love isn't who you can see yourself with, it's who you can't see yourself without.

Everyone hears what you have to say. Friends listen to what you say. Best friends listen to what you don't say.

You don't learn anything by doin' everything right.

Character is how you treat those who can do nothin' for you.

How far we travel in life matters far less than those we meet along the way.

When you get to be my age, a measure of success is lookin' back on your life and bein' able to smile.

I always looked at acquirin' a dog as one of the few opportunities I'd ever get to choose a relative.

Talk is cheap... 'cause supply exceeds demand.

Break ups aren't always meant for make ups. Sometimes relationships end in order for you to wake up.

Just because you can explain it doesn't mean it's not still a miracle.

Live your life in such a way that if anyone were to speak badly of you, no one would believe 'em.

A friend is one who believes in you when you cease to believe in yourself.

Everyone is entitled to be a little stupid now and then, but you'll be surprised how many abuse the privilege.

Women always worry about the things that men forget; but men always worry about the things that women remember.

Friendship is like good health, it's value is seldom known until it is lost.

If you don't think little things bother you, try sleepin' in a tent with a single mosquito.

Friends are those rare people who ask how you are and then wait to hear the answer.

The dictionary is the only place that "success" comes before "work".

The saddest moment in a person's life can only come once.

Sometimes, a road is less traveled for a reason.

They say a well-adjusted person is one who can make the same mistake twice without gettin' nervous.

Prejudices are like rats, and men's minds are like traps; prejudices get in easily, but it is doubtful if they ever get out.

The 1st Amendment to the US Constitution allows you to say what you think even if you don't think.

Promises are like cryin' babies in a theater, they should be carried out at once.

Don't cry because a romance has ended, smile because it happened.

Always pray for a tough hide and a tender heart.

Smile a lot, it makes people wonder what you're thinkin'.

Tryin' to do something and failin' is better than tryin' to do nothin' and succeedin'.

Somedays, you just have to create your own sunshine.

Life is a balance of holding on and lettin' go.

You can fail at something many times, but you're not a failure until you give up.

Nobody can go back and start a new beginnin', but anyone can start today and make a new endin'.

Only those who are asleep make no mistakes.

The value of consistent prayer is not that He will hear us, but that we will hear Him.

Age doesn't always bring wisdom, sometimes age comes alone.

Ask the Lord to help you resist temptation, especially when you know no one is lookin'.

Sometimes it isn't what you do, but what you don't do that makes you who you are.

If you don't have all the things you want, thank God for the things you don't have that you wouldn't want.

Make sure the important people in your life always know how important they are before it's too late.

God gave us love and lent us the rest.

You are what you think, not what you think you are.

If you treat every situation as a life and death matter, you'll die a lot of times.

The secret of contentment is the realization that life is a gift, not a right.

Coincidences are God's way of remainin' anonymous.

Someday your life may flash before your eyes, only you can make sure it's worth watchin'.

It isn't the hills in life that wear you out, it's the grain of sand in your boot.

I've found that the older I get, the list of things I'm supposed to " know better than" gets shorter and shorter.

Remember when you see a man at the top of a mountain, he didn't fall there.

Attitudes are contagious. Make sure yours is worth catchin'.

Life will always test you, but remember; when you walk up a mountain, your legs get stronger.

No relationship is ever a waste of time. If it didn't bring you what you want, it taught you what you didn't want.

It's far better to have a life filled with "oh wells" than a life filled with "what ifs".

Never wrestle with a pig. You both get dirty, but the pig likes it.

Children seldom misquote you. In fact, they usually repeat word for word what you shouldn't have said.

What we usually pray to God is not that His will be done, but that He approve ours.

The reason a dog has so many friends is that he wags his tail instead of his tongue.

The trouble with self-made men is that they tend to worship their creator.

A relationship with no arguments is usually a relationship with a lot of secrets.

Commitment means doin' what you said you were goin' to do long after the mood you said it in has left you.

Teach your children how to think, not what to think.

Everybody deserves somebody who makes them look forward to tomorrow.

The only gal you need in your life is the one that proves she needs you enough to be in hers.

Remember all relationships go through hard times but real relationships get through them.

A fool may talk, but a wise man speaks.

You can't start the next chapter of your life if you keep re-readin' the last one.

The journey in between what you started out as and who you are now becomin' is where the dance of life really takes place.

"Grief is a process, not an event—and it does not keep a schedule". (Corrie Sirota)

The ultimate test of a relationship is to disagree and still hold hands.

The strongest people are not those who show strength in front of us, but those who win battles we know nothin' about.

 Children are the livin' messages we send to a time we will never see.

Forget what hurt you, but never forget what it taught you.

Tough times don't last, tough people do. When the goin' gets tough, the tough get goin'.

A river cuts through a rock not because of its power, but its persistence.

Every experience, no matter how bad it seems, holds a blessin' of some kind. The goal is to find it.

When life is sweet, say thank you and celebrate. And when life is bitter, say thank you and grow.

The only way to limit your disappointments is to lower your expectations. But don't.

Eventually all of the pieces of your life will fall into place. Until then, laugh at the confusion, live for the moment, and know that everything happens for a reason.

Your mind will quit a thousand times before your body will. Feel the fear and do it.

Apologizin' doesn't always mean you're wrong, it just means that you value relationships more than your ego.

Mistakes don't matter as much as how you deal with 'em, what you learn from 'em, and how you apply that lesson to your life.

I have come to realize that most of life is simply repetition, a round of dull, uninspirin', lackluster things we must do again and again. But always remember that repetition is the mother of learnin'.

No matter how busy you are, always save time for your families, the one you were born into and the one you create for yourself.

If I had my life to live over, perhaps I'd have more actual troubles, but I'd dang sure have fewer imaginary ones.

Never make permanent decisions on temporary feelins'.

Time is free, but it's priceless. You can't own it, but you can use it, you can spend it, but you can't keep it. Once you've lost it, you can never get it back.

I've learned that people usually forget what you said, often forget what you did, but will never forget how you made them feel.

For a long time I used to think the worst thing in life was to end up all alone. It's not. The worst thing in life is to end up with people that make you feel all alone.

If you want to know where your heart is look to where your mind goes when it wanders.

Respect is earned. Honesty is appreciated. Trust is gained. Loyalty is returned.

Everything happens for a reason, except for the things you mess up yourself.

Your goal shouldn't be to live forever, but to create something that will.

To succeed in life, you need three things: a wishbone, a backbone, and a funny bone.

You'll never leave where you are until you decide where you want to be.

It's easy to become so focused on the finish line, that we fail to find joy in the journey.

What screws us up most in life is the picture in our head of how it's supposed to be.

I believe there is a purpose for every person you meet. Some will test you, some will use you, some will teach you, and some will bring out the worst in you, while others bring out the best.

Somethings are not meant to be understood, just accepted.

Usually people don't really change, they just reveal who they really are.

Always try to smile more than you cry, give more than you take, and love more than you hate.

Life's a climb, but the view is great.

Only by perseverance did the snails reach the ark.

I've been down on my luck a time or two and thanked God many times just for mac and cheese.

The older you get, the more you'll come to realize that the things that cost nothing hold the most value.

Don't be afraid to change, you may lose something good, but you may gain something better.

Every minute you spend with someone special gives them a part of your life and you a part of theirs.

In life, you are going to be lied to, left out, talked about and used, but you have to decide whose worth your tears and who ain't.

Live for accomplishments, not compliments.

As tough as it might be to accept, not all goodbyes only mean until tomorrow.

Lose the fear of being wrong.

One of the hardest things in life is to know which bridges to cross and which ones to burn.

You may not always end up where you thought you were goin', but you will always end up where you were meant to be.

We don't see things as they are, we see them as we are.

The only people who truly know your story are the ones that helped you write it.

When things go wrong, take a moment and thank God for the things goin' right.

Never trade what you want the most for what you want at the moment.

Sometimes the Lord washes our eyes out with tears so that we can see life with a clearer view again.

Some people truly believe that they can do anything they set their mind to, I wonder if they ever tried kissin' their elbow?

If you know better, you'll do better.

Life's problems wouldn't be called "hurdles" if there wasn't a way to get over them.

The hardest part of growin' up is lettin' go of what you were used to, and movin' on with something you're not.

Never let the things you want make you forget the things you already have.

A path with no obstacles probably won't lead you anywhere worth bein'.

Sometimes you fail at something because you don't know how close you were to succeedin' when you gave up.

Watch out for people who are always braggin' about who they are. A lion will never have to tell you it's a lion.

No, chickens do not have fingers.

What you see depends mostly on what you're lookin' for.

It's far better to be hurt by the truth than comforted with a lie.

I believe God doesn't give you the people you want in life, he gives you the people you need. To help you, to hurt you, to leave you, to love you and to make you into the person you were meant to be.

When you grow up I hope you can believe that you did all the wrong things, for all the right reasons. I'm still wonderin' about myself.

You'll never know how really strong you really are until being strong is the only choice you have.

I always wanted a perfect endin'. But now I've learned the hard way that some poems don't rhyme, and some stories don't have a clear beginnin', middle, or end. Life is about not knowin', havin' to change, takin' a moment and makin' the best of it without knowin' what's to happen next.

If I could make only one wish, it would be to not have a reason to make one.

Be the type of person you would like to meet.

Most often in life, we forget the things we should remember, and remember the things we should forget.

Never tell your problems to anyone. 80% don't care and 20% are glad they're your problems and not theirs.

You cannot change the people around you, but you can always change the people you choose to be around.

When writin' the story of your life, don't let anyone else hold the pen.

More people could learn from their mistakes if they weren't so busy denyin' 'em.

Try and remember that your character is made by many acts, but it can be destroyed by a single one.

The grass is only greener on the other side if you're not afraid to climb the fence.

Givin' up doesn't always mean you're weak, sometimes it means you're strong enough to let go.

Most everyone thinks of changin' the world now and then, but no one ever thinks of changin' themselves.

There'll come a time in your life when you think you've just about seen everything. I felt that way too, then heck, I remembered I've never seen a turtle jump.

Don't chase people. Be an example and attract them.

Faith is not about everything turnin' out OK; Faith is about bein' OK no matter how things turn out."

Always remember that only dead fish "go with the flow".

It's not important to be better than everybody else, but it's darn important to try and be better than you ever thought you could be.

The only expectations you should live up to are the ones you expect of yourself.

Don't let people's compliments get to your head and don't let their criticism get to your heart.

You should never regret the things you did wrong, only regret the good things you did for the wrong people.

If you can't be kind, be quiet.

It's much better to walk alone than in a crowd goin' in the wrong direction.

You change for two reasons. Either you learn enough that you want to or you've been hurt enough that you have to.

Don't ever stray away from yourself to get closer to someone else.

You will have days when you feel your luck has run out and it's you against the world. When that happens, remember that God loves each of us as if there was only one of us.

A pretty face doesn't mean a pretty heart.

Keep in mind how hard it is to change yourself and you'll understand how difficult it is to change others.

A good friend knows all your stories. A best friend helped you write them.

Sometimes you have to lose who you were to find out who you are.

Right is right, even if no one is doing it. Wrong is wrong, even if everyone is doing it.

You'll never become who you want to be if you keep blamin' everyone else for who you are.

Be a strong voice, not an echo.

Don't spend a lot of time worryin' too much about people who don't worry none about you.

Speak in such a way that others love to listen to you. Listen in such a way that others love to speak to you.

A lion doesn't lose sleep over the opinions of sheep.

Remember that people will always question the good things they hear about you, and believe the bad ones without a second thought.

Worry is a down payment on a problem you may never have.

Listen to people when they are angry, 'cause that's usually when the real truth comes out.

If you characterize people by their actions and you'll never be fooled by their words.

It's not about who is real to your face, it's about who stays loyal behind your back.

Never trust your tongue when your heart is bitter.

The people in your life that are quick to walk away are the ones who never intended to stay in the first place.

Only those who care about you can hear you when you're quiet.

No one ever makes himself look important by makin' someone else look unimportant.

Don't ever try and gain attention for yourself by losin' respect for yourself.

When I was your age, I often wished to be older so I could do those things that only older people could. Now I am older, much older and it's not what I expected; I often catch myself wishin' to be young again. Live every day to the fullest and don't wish your life away.

True friendship is when two friends can walk in opposite directions, yet remain side by side.

Never mix bad words with your bad mood. You'll have many chances to change a mood, but you'll never get the chance to replace the words.

Don't ever judge someone just because they sin differently than you do.

Sometimes silence is more powerful than having the last word.

Holding onto anger is like drinkin' poison and expectin' the other person to die.

Worry about your character, not your reputation. Your character is who you are. Your reputation is who people think you are.

People are probably not happy with their own life if they're busy talkin' about yours.

When you throw dirt, you lose ground.

One thing you can do better than anyone else, is be yourself.

Her beauty might get your attention but it's her personality that will get your heart.

You are only responsible for what you say, not for what others hear and understand.

Bein' nice to someone you'd rather slap isn't bein' phony, it's suckin' it up and actin' like an adult.

Sometimes, lyin' in bed at night, I Iook back on my life and find comfort and satisfaction in thinkin' that if I had it to do all over again, there's not a whole lot I would change. I hope someday, you both can look back on your lives and feel the same.

Never argue with an idiot. He'll drag you down to his level and beat you with experience.

If you think too much, you'll create a problem that wasn't even there in the first place.

If ketchup, jalapenos or Tobasco sauce don't fix it, don't eat it

It's better to lose an argument to someone, than lose someone to an argument.

True friendship isn't about bein' inseparable, it's being separated and nothing changes.

If you don't actually see it with your own eyes, don't invent it with your mouth.

The people who know the least about you are usually the ones who have the most to say.

Haters will scream your failures and whisper your successes.

Don't let people mistake your silence for ignorance, your calmness for acceptance, or your kindness for weakness.

Never let your ears witness what your eyes didn't see, or let your mouth speak what your heart doesn't feel.

Sometimes you'll hear what others have done, but rarely do you hear what others have been through. Don't judge !

It's wise to taste your words before you spit them out.

You'll find the hardest thing about two-faced people is decidin' which face to slap first.

Respect other people's feelins' even if it doesn't mean anything to you, it could mean everything to them.

Sometimes the people you'd take a bullet for, are the ones behind the trigger.

The person who thinks too little usually talks too much.

Good friends will always help you find the important things when you've lost them; your smile, your hope, and your courage.

Most people know how to say nothin'; but damn few know when.

Wisdom is divided into two parts, having a great deal to say, and not saying it.

No individual raindrop ever considers itself responsible for the flood.

If you ever feel that you are indispensable, put your finger in a glass of water, then pull it out and look at the hole that remains.

Never try to teach a pig to think. You'll never succeed and it annoys the pig.

Nothing is more humblin' than that moment during an argument when you realize you're wrong.

I never could figure out how one careless match can start a forest fire, but it takes a whole box to start a campfire?

You can tell a man there are 300 billion stars in the universe and he'll believe you. Tell him a bench has wet paint on it and he'll have to touch it to be sure.

I've laid awake at night several times wonderin' why Noah didn't swat those two mosquitoes?

The good Lord gave you a shinbone to remind you that you left the ball in the receiver hitch on the back of your pick-up. He thinks of everything !

Holdin' on to anger is like graspin' a hot coal with the intent of throwin' it at someone else; you're the only one who gets burned.

When you're a father, you'll carry pictures in your wallet where your money used to be.

If the facts don't back up the story, you can always change 'em.

The way I figure, it all went to hell when attacking what we hate became more important than defendin' what we love.

Fallin' in love is like jumpin' off a really tall cliff. Your brain tells you it is not a good idea, but your heart tells you, you can fly.

Death leaves a heartache no one can heal, but love leaves a memory no one can steal.

You know, If nothin' ever changed, there'd be no butterflies.

You'll learn much from your teachers, more from your books, but most from your mistakes.

If science finally locates the center of the universe, you'll be amazed how many people you know will be surprised to learn they're not it.

I've always thought that if you try and forget a woman you loved, you probably never really loved her to begin with.

Not that I'm braggin', but I've kissed my share of women in my time, some blushed when they were kissed, some swore, some bit, and a couple even called the sheriff. But the ones that bothered me the worst were the ones who laughed.

I've determined that the fewer facts you have in support of an opinion, the stronger your emotional attachment to that opinion.

Don't ever be afraid to ask dumb questions; they're easier to handle than dumb mistakes.

You won't find any cuisine at the café in town, they only serve regular food. Cuisine is what some restaurants call food so they can serve you less and charge you more.

The soul would have no rainbow if the eye had no tears.

Long ago, I worked with an Indian fella who always said, "Those that lie down with dogs, get up with fleas". I always remembered that when it came to makin' new friends. You would be wise to do the same.

An accountant is a person you hire to explain that you didn't make the money you thought you did.

You know you can't make someone love you. All you can do is be someone who can be loved. The rest is up to them.

"There are some people who, if they don't already know, you can't tell 'em." (Yogi Berra)

It's easy to have courage from a long way off.

You can't be one person on Sunday and another on Monday without God knowin' it. He checks his pastures every day.

Every bird loves to hear himself sing.

The Lord is responsible for makin' everything, but he won't make you love him....that's up to you.

Just because someone doesn't love you the way you want them to, doesn't mean they don't love you with all they have.

A long time ago, I learned that you can get by on charm for about fifteen minutes; after that, you'd better know somethin'.

Be careful with the one you love, you can do something in an instant that will give you heartache for life.

It's always been a lot easier to react than it is to think.

Even a tiny mouse has a temper.

Learnin' to forgive takes practice.

Most of us don't look as handsome to others as we do to ourselves.

There are people who love you dearly, but just don't know how to show it.

Money is a lousy way of keepin' score.

Sometimes you may have every right to be angry, but that never gives you the right to be cruel.

Maturity has more to do with what types of experiences you've had and what you've learned from 'em and less to do with how many birthdays you've celebrated.

Never tell a child their dreams are silly or outlandish. Few things are more humiliatin', and what a tragedy it would be if they believed it.

Just because two people argue, doesn't mean they don't love each other. And just because they don't argue, doesn't mean they do.

They call 'em Rocky Mountain Oysters only 'cause it sounds more appitizin' than Bull Nuts. I've also heard 'em called Montana Tendergroin, Cowboy Caviar, Bull Berrys and Bull Fries. Whatever you call 'em they sure are tasty. Grandma just wrinkles her nose at 'em.

Families don't have to be biological.

It's a good idea to load your brain before shootin' your mouth off.

You shouldn't be so eager to find out a secret. It could change your life forever.

Two people can look at the exact same thing and see something totally different.

Just because you have credentials on the wall do not make you a decent human bein'.

I've learned the hard way that it's difficult to determine where to draw the line between bein' nice and not hurtin' people's feelins' and still standin' up for what you believe.

Indian folks are usually people of few words, but when they do speak, they usually say something pretty profound. I once heard one say, "It is better to have less thunder in the mouth and more lightning in the hand." Think about that. Actions speak louder than words.

People like to refer to "life" by many different names. I've heard it referred to as a game, a dance, a party, a book, a hill to climb, a journey to take, a road, and the list goes on and on. But I think the best analogy came from an old friend of mine who referred to life as a baseball game. It's filled with fastballs, sliders, curves and screwballs. You get hits, make errors and occasionally hit a homerun. You lose more games than you win, and some get rained out, but you have to suit up for 'em all; just don't forget to wear your cup. I think he summed it up pretty well.

Everyone has troubles in their life from time to time, don't let it get you down. Most troubles are like raindrops, they don't pick and choose who they land on.

Worry is like tryin' to ride down the trail with your saddle on backwards. You might get there eventually, but you've sure made life difficult on yourself.

I hope you don't ever have to tell someone you're a Christian. It should be so obvious by the way you live that they don't even have to wonder.

When someone says that they agree with somethin' in principle, they really mean that they don't have the slightest intention of carryin' it out in practice.

I've found that advice is like castor oil, easy to give, but dreadful to take.

The rain falls on the just and the unjust. (Matthew 5:45)

If you can't see any reason for givin' the Lord thanks, the fault lies in yourself.

When you see frog legs on a restaurant menu, yes, they are really frog legs, but buffalo wings ain't really buffalo wings.

Friends never say, "I told you so." They stand there grinnin' and never say a word.

When you're in the pasture herdin' cattle, the only time papers on a horse really means something is when they're white and come on a roll.

Three phrases you should throw away are: I want, I think, and I know.

Settin' fence posts all day will sure make you grateful that we can only get to heaven by grace and not by works

Bein' able to do anything ain't the same as bein' able to do everything. You should learn the difference.

It is one thing puttin' away the past, and quite another to tape its mouth shut.

Someday you'll learn the thing that counts most in the pursuit of happiness is choosin' the right companion.

The only difference between stumblin' blocks and steppin' stones is how you use them.

Always be nice to people on your way up 'cause you meet them again on your way down.

If you want to test your memory, try to remember what you were worryin' about one year ago today.

Sleep is an excellent way of listening to an opera.

Advice is what you ask for when you already know the answer but wish you didn't.

Always forgive your enemies, but never forget their names.

Sometimes only the questions are complicated but the answers are simple.

I guess I'm not really afraid of death; I just don't want to be there when it happens.

If you don't tell the truth, someone else will tell it for you.

A learnin' experience is one of those things that says, "I shouldn't have done what I just did."

I'll try anything once, twice if I like it, three times just to make sure.

A soldier doesn't fight 'cause he hates what's in front of him, but 'cause he loves what's behind him.

Christianity ain't about what you're not doin' anymore....it's about what yer doin' now.

You can have money piled to the ceiling but the size of your funeral is still going to depend on the weather.

It seems ironic that you can die for someone, but couldn't and wouldn't live for them.

There's a heck of a lot more to manhood than beards and chest hair.

You'll learn one day that the best advice is the advice that doesn't interfere with what you intended to do in the first place.

A dog is one of the few things on earth that loves you more than you love yourself.

The only time age matters is if you're cheese.

You'll never learn anything from a man who agrees with you.

The trouble with not havin' a goal is that you can spend your life runnin' up and down the field and never score.

Friends may come and go in your life, but enemies seem to accumulate.

Just 'cause you found 100 ways to do somethin' that won't work, doesn't mean you failed.

A memory is what's left when somethin' happens and don't completely un-happen.

Defeat is not bitter unless you swallow it.

Some people feel the rain, others just get wet.

The truth will set you free. But first, it usually makes you very angry.

I've often wondered if I spoke in the forest and your grandma wasn't there to hear me, would I still be wrong?

Your children need your presence more than your presents.

The best thing to take for a short temper is a long walk.

I've read somewhere that an alligator is a much faster swimmer than a human, and can also outrun us on land. So if you ever enter a triathlon against an alligator, you'd better build up a huge lead in the bicyclin' event.

If winnin' isn't everything then why do people keep score?

You'll learn in school that light travels faster than sound... that's probably why most people might appear brilliant until you hear 'em speak.

There are two kinds of people, those who do the work, and those who take the credit. Try to be in the first group; there is less competition there.

Only men think "multi-tasking" is siitin' on a toilet readin' a magazine.

Jesus wants you to know he registered a brand about 2,000 years ago. It is the "4U".

I've seen sorrow, happiness, curiosity, and wonder all in the sideways tilt of a dog's head. If they can say so much with so little why can't we? Actions speak so much louder than words.

A true friend is not afraid to say something to you that you're afraid to say to yourself.

You never get a second chance to make a first impression

A real optimist is a cowboy who gets throw'd from his horse, treed by a mountain lion and still enjoys the scenery from his vantage point.

You can't go through life wearin' a catcher's mitt on both yer hands. There will come a time when you have to throw somethin' back.

If we are facing in the right direction, all we have to do is keep on walking.

When your heart is talking, there are no wrong words.

Don't confuse action with motion they are not synonymous.

Don't be discouraged ,it's often the last key in the bunch that opens the lock.

Next in importance to having a good aim is knowin' when to pull the trigger.

Don't worry that children never listen to you; worry that they are always watchin' you.

Big shots are only little shots who kept shootin'.

Although there are many trial marriages... there is no such thing as a trial child.

If you want to forget all your other troubles, wear boots that are too tight.

A trail with no obstacles, probably doesn't lead anywhere.

Although you may not realize it when it happens, but sometimes a good, swift kick in the seat may be the best thing in the world for you.

When your mom or grandma asks, "Do you want a piece of advice?" it's a mere formality. It doesn't matter if you answer yes or no. You're goin' to get it anyway.

My folks always taught me to respect my elders but I've now reached the age when an elder is getting' harder and harder to find.

The first sign of maturity is the discovery that the volume knob on the radio in your pick-up also turns to the left.

Some questions in life never get answered, like why does a dog turn around three times before lyin' down?

Any child can tell you that the sole purpose of a middle name is so he can tell when he's really in trouble.

You know you're getting' old when you never get the urge to throw a snowball.

When I was a younger man, I spent most of my money on women and beer, the rest I just wasted.

Politics is the gentle art of getting' votes from the poor and campaign funds from the rich, by promisin' to protect each from the other.

Bein' meek doesn't mean surrenderin' to the will of man, but to the will of God.

What a child doesn't receive he can seldom later give.

Most people never run far enough on their first wind to find out they've got a second.

I've never been able to figure out why none of the men in beer commercials has a beer belly.

Never lose sight of the fact that alcoholism isn't a spectator sport. Eventually your whole family gets to play.

It appears we have finally reached gender equality, 'cause we can elect women to public office who are just as incompetent as some of the men who are already there.

I am ashamed to admit that I spent most of my prayer life askin' God to take care of the things that were breakin' my heart, when I should have been prayin' about the things that were breakin' His heart.

Speak when you are angry and you will usually make the best speech you'll ever regret.

What I like about dogs is that they come when they're called; cats on the other hand, take a message and get back to you later.

If you have never been hated by your child you have never been a parent.

People are a lot like birds: some fly high in the sky, while others fly into windows.

It don't matter how old your mother is, or how old you are, she will always be watchin' you for signs of improvement. That's just what mothers do.

Children have never been very good at listenin' to their elders, but they have never failed to imitate them to perfection.

A successful life doesn't require that you've done the best, but that you've done your best.

Courage ain't always about ridin' the biggest, meanest bull, sometimes courage is the little voice at the end of the day that says I'll try again tomorrow.

Dogs never talk about themselves but always listen to you while you're talkin' about yourself, and they even manage to keep up an appearance of bein' interested in the entire conversation.

God retains editing rights over your prayers. He will... edit them, correct them, bring them in line with His will and then hand them back to you to be resubmitted.

Parenthood is a lot easier to get into than out of.

A hen is about the only thing that ever sits its way to success.

Men are usually made stronger when they come to the realization that the helpin' hand they need is at the end of their own arm.

Effort is like toothpaste: you can usually squeeze out just a little bit more.

It's probably good that dogs can't talk, or perhaps we'd find it as hard to get along with them as we get along with people.

Conservatives believe in equality of opportunity. Liberals believe in equality of outcome.

Although I think it's a kin to lyin' to deliberately exaggerate when you're tellin' a story, I think it's perfectly acceptable to remember big.

A good man never makes excuses, a smart man never puts himself in a position to need one.

You don't have to be the biggest to beat the biggest.

A man who carries a cat by the tail learns something he can't learn any other way.

Education is what you get when you read the fine print. Experience is what you get if you don't.

Learn all you can from the mistakes of others. You won't have time to make 'em all yourself.

I don't agree with the Democrat's notion that those who are equal in any respect are equal in all respects.

The only thing more painful than learnin' from experience, is not learnin' from experience.

You don't fail because you lose, you fail because you give up.

A father is a man who expects his children to be as good as he meant to be.

"It's easier said than done" is the most trite excuse ever uttered. Don't use it!

A man begins cuttin' his wisdom teeth the first time he bites off more than he can chew.

Integrity is tellin' yourself the truth. And honesty is tellin' the truth to other people.

It don't matter how bad your memory gets, nobody ever forgets where he buried the hatchet.

Experience is that marvelous thing that enables you to recognize a mistake when you've made it twice.

When a fellow says it ain't the money but the principle of the thing, it's the money.

A bank is a place where they lend you an umbrella in fair weather and ask for it back when it begins to rain.

Money may talk, but have you ever noticed how hard of hearing it is when you call it.

There are no illegitimate children only illegitimate parents.

A "young man" is really a little boy who has just done something dreadful.

Parents often talk about the younger generation as if they didn't have anything to do with it.

The difference between success and failure is persistence.

I believe ice cream is clearly God's way of sayin' that He likes us a little chubby.

Moms and grandmas give the kind of hugs where you can feel the sadness leavin' your body. It's good to hug 'em often.

Tryin' to push a little God into your life is like pushin' a rope. It goes everywhere except where you want it to. But if you turn it around and put God first and let Him lead the way, your life will line up right behind Him just right.

Old age is havin' a lot of crossed off names in your address book.

Prejudice is neither a symptom of hatred, nor stupidity. It is merely a symptom of ignorance.

You should never name an animal that's not yours to keep, or that you intend to eat.

I have long considered it one of God's greatest mercies that the future is hidden from us. If it were not, life would surely be unbearable.

Patriotism is your conviction that this country is superior to all other countries simply because you were born in it.

Nothin' makes you more tolerant of a neighbor's noisy party than bein' there.

Every saint has a past and every sinner has a future.

I truly believe that everything happens for a reason, the hardest part is waiting for that reason to show up.

The 10 Commandments contain 297 words. The Bill of Rights is stated in 463 words. Lincoln's Gettysburg Address contains 266 words. A recent federal directive to regulate the price of cabbage contains 26,911 words. Draw your own conclusion.

The closest to perfection a person ever comes is when he fills out a job application form.

The main thing is to keep the main thing the main thing.

I read once that age, nutrition, and genetics determine the size of a buck deer's rack. When I told that to your grandma she replied that all age, nutrition and genetics got me was a big belly. She was only kiddin', I think. Later she told me that if I was a buck deer, I'd be a trophy. Hell, I knew that!

Promises are like cryin' babies in a theater, they should be carried out at once.

Too often we give children answers to remember rather than problems to solve.

It galls me that a citizen of America will cross the ocean to fight for democracy, but won't cross the street to vote in a national election.

You can't play the game of life with sweaty palms.

People demand freedom of speech to make up for the freedom of thought which they avoid.

In the game of life nothin' is less important than the score at half time.

What we see depends mainly on what we look for.

Always try and pick battles big enough to matter, but small enough to win.

Failures are sorta' like skinned knees; painful, but superficial and never life threatin'.

The greatest man in history was the poorest.

Lookin' back, seems all the things I really liked to do were either immoral, illegal or fattenin'.

You can't really enjoy the better things in life, until you've experienced the things they are better than.

The reason there are so few female politicians is that it is too much trouble to put makeup on two faces.

Prayer gives a man the opportunity of gettin' to know a gentleman he hardly ever meets. No, not his maker, but himself.

You haven't converted a man just because you've silenced him.

It would be foolish to let a fox sit on the jury of a rabbit.

No man is born with prejudices, they are a product of his own experiences. No one can eliminate them, just recognize them.

My mother always told me I wouldn't amount to anything because I procrastinate. I said, "Just wait".

Losers make promises they seldom keep, winners make commitments they always keep.

A fella who feeds on praise is always hungry.

I believe most people are rude on purpose, not by accident.

People are usually very open-minded about new things as long as they're exactly like the old ones.

Happiness isn't destination to arrive at, but a manner of travelin'.

Courage is contagious. When a brave man takes a stand, the spines of others are stiffened.

When a sorrow comes our way, we have no right to ask, "Why did this happen to me?" unless we ask the same question for every joy that comes our way.

Faith is not belief without proof, but trust without reservation.

Happiness is like a kiss...you must share it to enjoy it.

When I was a younger man, I asked God for strength and He gave me difficulties to make me strong. I asked Him for wisdom and He gave me problems to solve. I asked God for prosperity and He gave me brawn and brains to work. I asked for courage and He gave me dangers to overcome. I prayed for patience and He put me in situations where I was forced to wait. I asked Him for love and He gave me troubled people to help. I asked for favors and He gave me opportunities. I asked for all things, that I might enjoy life, I was given life, that I might enjoy all things ... I got nothin' that I asked for, but everything I'd hoped for. Almost despite myself, my unspoken prayers were answered. I am among all men, most richly blessed.

Don't be reckless with other people's hearts, and don't put up with those who are reckless with yours.

The first rule to tinkerin' is to save all the parts.

Always and never are two words you should always remember never to use.

Democracy is a form of government in which it is permitted to wonder aloud what the country could do under first-class management

What can you say about a society that says God is dead and Elvis is alive?

The person who says "I won't say another word" always does.

The great thing about gettin' older is that you don't lose all the other ages you've been.

Failure can be divided into those who thought and never did and those who did and never thought.

I always give myself great advice, but seldom take it.

Courage can't see around corners, but goes around 'em anyway.

Whenever I reach heaven I expect to find three wonders there: first, to meet some I had never thought to see there; second, to miss some I had expected to see there; and third, the greatest wonder of all, to find myself there.

A hug is the perfect gift; one size fits all, and nobody minds if you exchange it.

Be a good listener. Your ears will never get you in trouble.

I wish there was a knob on the TV to turn up the intelligence. There's a knob called 'brightness,' but it doesn't work either.

I'd rather have a moment of wonderful than a lifetime of nothing special.

If somethin' is real important to you or your family, then make things happen, don't just sit back and let things happen. Never grow a wishbone where a backbone ought to be.

There are two types of people: those who GET IT and those who DON'T. If they GET IT, there's nothin' to explain and if they DON'T, there's no point in tryin' to explain.

The attempt to silence a man is the greatest honor you can bestow on him. It means that you recognize his superiority over you.

The most important trip you may take in life is meetin' people halfway.

Seems we always want the facts to fit the assumptions. When they don't, it is easier to ignore the facts than to change the assumptions.

God gave us memory so that we might have roses in December.

You will learn that "oh, what the hell" is usually the right decision?

Threats don't work with the person who's got nothin' to lose.

Why would most of us like to be smarter than we are, stronger than we are, richer than we are, but we don't feel all that comfortable bein' around people who are?

Tradition is what you resort to when you don't have the time or the money to do it right.

A man never stands as tall as when he kneels to help a child.

Life is like a dogsled team. If you ain't the lead dog, the scenery never changes.

You're not the only one who's made mistakes, but they're the only things that you can truly call your own.

A synonym is a word you use when you can't spell the word you first thought of.

The best way to have a good idea is to have a lot of 'em. Eventually the law of averages will catch up to you.

Try and be decisive, make a decision and stand by it. The road of life is littered with flattened squirrels that couldn't make a decision.

There is nobody so irritatin' as somebody with less intelligence and more sense than you have.

Isn't it surprisin' how many things, if not said immediately, seem not worth sayin' ten minutes later?

Silent gratitude isn't much use to anyone.

Progress always involves risk; you can't steal second base while keepin' your foot on first base.

The person who knows how will always have a job. The person who knows why will always be his boss.

People usually forget how fast you did a job -- but they always remember how well you did it.

The only difference between a rut and a grave is the depth.

Don't be afraid to take a big step if one is necessary, you can't cross a 20 foot gully in two 10 foot jumps.

People are more easily led than driven.

A diplomat is a person who can tell you to go to hell in such a way that you actually look forward to the trip.

The key to being a good boss is keepin' the people who hate you away from those who are still undecided.

It's amazin' how nice people are to you when they know you're going away.

Always read stuff that will make you look good in case you die in the middle of it.

"Automatic" simply means that you can't repair it yourself.

Experience is somethin' you don't get until just after you need it.

You're never as good as everyone tells you when you win, and you're never as bad as they say when you lose either.

We judge ourselves by what we feel capable of doin', while others judge us by what we have already done.

Democracy is a process by which the people are free to choose the person who will get the blame.

I don't necessarily agree with everything I say.

If everything's under control, you're probably goin' too slow.

Just think how happy you would be if you lost everything you have right now, and then got it all back again.

A statesman is a politician who places himself at the service of the nation. A politician is a statesman who places the nation at his service.

Sometimes I wish I hadn't been in such a hurry to move forward. There comes a point when it becomes impossible to go back

I've always wondered if committin' a crime is the same as failin' to comply with the law?

You can't teach people to be lazy - either they have it, or they don't.

You'd be wise to observe the turtle. He makes progress only when he sticks his neck out.

If a thing goes without sayin' -- let it.

Sometimes it's difficult to distinguish between the unfortunate and the incompetent.

Most things don't go wrong, they simply happen.

There's no fool like an old fool -- you can't beat experience.

A vacation is what you take when you can't take what you've been takin' any longer.

We're all proud of makin' little mistakes. It gives us the feelin' we don't make any big ones.

If you are goin' to walk on thin ice you might as well dance!

The next best thing to winning is losing! At least you've been in the race.

Don't do to others what would anger you if done to yourself.

Begin somewhere; you cannot build a reputation on what you intend to do.

I think adults are always askin' kids what they want to be when they grow up 'cause they are lookin' for ideas.

The simple act of payin' attention can take you a long way.

The only reason some people get lost in thought is because it's unfamiliar territory.

About the only time losin' is more fun than winnin' is when you're fightin' temptation.

I have had more trouble with myself than with any other man I've met.

Experience is what you get when you don't get what you want.

A loser doesn't know what he'll do if he loses, but talks about what he'll do if he wins, and a winner doesn't talk about what he'll do if he wins, but knows what he'll do if he loses.

Many people lose their tempers merely from seeing you keep yours.

Opportunity always looks bigger goin' than comin'.

Hit the ball over the fence and you can take your time going around the bases.

Many a man's tongue broke his nose.

Sometimes it's easier to get forgiveness than permission.

What we must decide is how we are valuable rather than how valuable we are.

Half of knowin' what you want is knowin' what you must give up to get it.

All of us could take a lesson from the weather, it pays no attention to criticism

Logic is a systematic method of comin' to the wrong conclusion with confidence.

When the collection plate passes in front of you, don't think that God needs your money, but you and I need the experience of giving it.

Holding on to anger only gives you tense muscles.

Time sneaks up on you like a windshield on a bug.

No man's life, liberty or property are safe while the legislature is in session.

Democracy encourages the majority to decide things about which the majority is ignorant.

A psychiatrist asks a lot of expensive questions your wife asks for nothin'.

Faith is not tryin' to believe something regardless of the evidence. Faith is darin' to do something regardless of the consequences

Discussion is an exchange of knowledge, arguments an exchange of ignorance.

Tact is the art of makin' guests feel at home when that's really where you wish they were.

You wouldn't worry what others think of you . . . If you knew how seldom they do!

What makes resistin' temptation difficult for many people is they don't really want to discourage it, at least completely.

Half of the American people have never read a newspaper. Half never voted for President. You can only hope it is the same half.

An adversary's silence is sufficient praise.

Never forget that a half truth is still a whole lie.

Even though we can't have all we want, we ought to be thankful we don't get what we deserve.

On occasion I've listened to sermons that reminded me of commercials, but I couldn't determine if God was the sponsor or the product.

There's one thing for which you should be abundantly thankful -- only you and God know all the facts about yourself.

Don't be content with bein' average. Average is as close to the bottom as it is to the top.

No one ever complains about a sermon being too short!

Just because someone is silent doesn't mean they're not screamin' inside.

Our elections are free--it's in the results where eventually we pay.

Accept that some days you're the pigeon and other days you're the statue.

I've learned a long time ago to never try and guess your grandma's size, I just buy her something marked "petite" and hold on to the receipt.

The door to opportunity is always labeled "push".

A friend is someone who knows the song in your heart and can sing it back to you when you have forgotten the words.

The more you know, the less you need to show.

I do believe in the 'Big Bang' theory, God spoke and 'BANG', it was.

A fellow can't keep people from havin' a bad opinion of him, but he can keep them from bein' right about it.

You know it's a bad day when you put your underwear on backwards and it fits better.

Sometimes a little inaccuracy saves a lot of explainin'.

I am sure there are many things better than smokin' a good cigar while sippin' some Drambuie; but right now, I can't think of what they might be.

Some people would rather look backward then forward, 'cause it's easier to remember where you've been than to figure out where you're goin'.

It's amazin'...you can be in a room with 100 girls and not like any one of 'em, but you can be in a room with one girl and know that she's the right one for you.

It's okay to talk to yourself, I do often, but just don't interrupt.

It's true that we don't know what we've got until we lose it, but it's also true that we don't know what we've been missin' until it arrives.

Don't blow out someone else's candle just to make yours look brighter.

Dancing with your feet is one thing, but dancing with your heart is another.

Always be mindful of your thoughts, they may become words at any moment.

"Influence" is a word used mostly by grownups, and it's a term I've often pondered. You can influence others, or you can be influenced by others. You can have influence and you can lend your influence. You can gain influence, and you can lose influence. Some people try to buy influence, while others peddle their influence. But I believe influence is more than lofty acts and words associated with wealth; it can be as simple as a smile, listenin' to others, lendin' a helpin' hand, lovin', and most often overlooked, prayin'.

Remember, people will judge you by your actions, not your intentions. You might think you have a heart of gold – but so does a hard-boiled egg.

A diplomat is a man who says you have an open mind, instead of telling you that you have a hole in the head.

It seems that when money talks, nobody cares about its grammar.

Hard work will never kill you, sweat is the only liquid In which you cannot drown.

Beware of the half-truth. You may have gotten hold of the wrong half.

The biggest danger with talkin' too fast is you may say something you haven't thought of yet.

Smile, it's the second best thing you can do with your lips.

God doesn't call us to be successful. He calls us to be faithful.

Lookin' back at my life, I can honestly say that I've never hated a man enough nor had the courage to ask the Lord to take his life. However, I must admit that I've given the Lord a fairly detailed list of names of those scoundrels I thought deserved a kidney stone or two.

Tact is the art of makin' a point without makin' an enemy.

Money can buy you knowledge, but not the wisdom to use it wisely.

You never know when you're makin' a memory.

I have a real fear that one day I'll meet God, He'll sneeze and I won't know what to say?

You'll run across people who want to share their religious views with you, but almost never want you to share yours with them.

Some days you're the dog, some days you're the hydrant.

Most of us can read the writin' on the wall; we just assume it's addressed to someone else.

Responsibility is saying "I lost it" instead of "It got lost".

Nothin' makes it easier to resist temptation than a proper up-bringin', a sound set of values and witnesses.

It ain't a bad plan to keep still occasionally even when you know what you're talkin' about.

After a truly fine meal, smokin' a fine cigar is still the most satisfyin' after dinner activity that don't involve two human beings.

Old men like me find a lot of satisfaction in plantin' trees whose shade we know we'll never sit in.

"Somebody once said there are only two kinds of people in the world. There are those who wake up in the morning and say, "Good mornin', Lord," and there are those who wake up in the morning and say, "Good Lord, it's mornin'."

Apologizin'' for something you know you're gonna' do again is a waste of good time and breath.

The secret to bein' a good speaker is to make sure you have finished speakin' before your audience has finished listenin'.

Always do sober what you said you'd do when you were drinkin'. That'll teach you to keep your mouth shut.

"How are you?" is a form of greetin', not a question. So when you hear it, don't start talkin' about all your physical ailments.

I have opinions of my own –strong ones too– but I don't always agree with 'em.

Bein' wise ain't that tough, just think of something stupid to say and then don't say it.

As I see it, 'bout the only problem with success is that it doesn't teach you how to deal with failure.

Sympathy is never wasted except when you give it to yourself.

When a teacher or your folks call you by your entire name, you're in trouble.

Don't pat yourself on the back for speakin' the truth, it's what you're supposed to do.

A proud man is seldom a grateful man, for he never thinks he gets as much as he deserves.

Why does nobody believe an official spokesman... but everybody believes an unidentified source?

You'll never know how far you can go, unless you try to go too far.

The fool wonders, the wise man asks.

Sometimes there is just no easy way, the hardest way is the only way.

How you win or lose is much more important than how much you win or lose.

Teachin' kids to count is fine, but teachin' them what counts is best.

Always be wary of a man who urges action but doesn't have a skin in the game.

You can tell more about a person by what he says about others than you can by what others say about him.

Concentration is the ability to think about absolutely nothin' when it is absolutely necessary.

Happiness has a way of sneakin' in through a door you didn't know you left open.

Money won't solve all your problems, it only lets you carry your unhappiness around in style.

Ever think about shadows? Without the presence of something real, there is no shadow to be cast. Shadows need something of substance in order to exist. The love you share with others is a shadow of Christ's love for you; and the forgiveness you offer to your neighbor is a shadow of Christ's forgiveness offered to you. Always try and remember that.

A wise man isn't someone who solves problems, truth is, a wise man is someone who avoids problems.

I prefer to call your grandma a "homemaker", 'cause "housewife" implies that there may be another wife someplace else.

Hard work doesn't guarantee success, but it improves its chances.

In youth we learn, but in old age we understand.

Moms and grandmas have a unique gift of understandin' what a child doesn't say.

Discipline is just choosin' between what you want now and what you want most

Imagination is somethin' that sits up with your folks the first time you stay out late.

I have often pondered which hurt me the most: sayin' somethin' and wishin' I hadn't, or sayin' nothin', and wishin' I had?"

The bitterest tears shed over graves are for words left unsaid and deeds left undone.

One of the hardest things in life is watchin' the person you love, love someone else."

 Although your schoolin' will end someday, your education never ends..

If your mom says "No", always appeal to your grandma.

Appreciate your mom. She is wiser than you think and stronger than you will ever know. Be thankful.

Get used to the fact that not everything can be controlled. Tears are good example; they have a mind of their own. You never intend to get weepy, but there they are, wettin' your cheeks.

I believe the saddest words in all of life are "if only". If only I……hadn't started smokin', said I was sorry, knew when I'd had enough to drink, spent more time with the kids, saw the doctor sooner, walked away, shut my mouth, planned for retirement, finished college, showered her with love and tenderness instead of unending criticism and scorn, had a close relationship with God. Yup, "if only" is an echo from your heart of past deeds we wish we could change or take back. I've uttered those two words to myself hundreds of times in my life and unfortunately you probably will too. When it happens, don't get down on yourself, make things right if you can and ask forgiveness for the things you can't, and let it go.

More likely than not, there will be times in your life when things just ain't goin' your way. Just remember "Even strong young lions sometimes go hungry" (Psalm 34).

I've always believed that a person who eagerly proclaims to have a clear conscience, usually has a fuzzy memory.

Always keep in mind that although you can't control the outcome of a situation, you are 100% in control of the effort.

Most liberals are usually willin' to listen to a different opinion, just as soon as they get over the shock that there could even be a different opinion.

If you can't fix it with duct tape, WD-40, pliers or a hammer, better call a repairman.

In the end... We only regret the chances we didn't take, the relationships we were afraid to have, and the decisions we waited too long to make. Don't waste a single moment.

Someday if you are blessed with children of your own, "don't educate them to be rich, educate them to be happy. So when they grow up they will know the value of things and not the price". (Steve Jobs)

Every morning, even before you get out of bed, whisper this simplest of prayers, "Dear God, Your will, nothing more, nothing less, nothing else, Amen." (Bobby Richardson)

I wish you boys a very long, prosperous and joyous life. Along the way you will surely have many trials and tribulations that will test your faith in God. As hard as it might be at times, always remember that He never says you won't have to go through them; but He promises that He'll be with you when you do. (Isaiah 41:10)

Psalm 118 is the very center of the Bible. There are 594 chapters before Psalm 118 and 594 chapters after Psalm 118. The center verse of the entire bible is Psalm 118:8, "It is better to take refuge in the Lord than to trust in man." No truer words were ever spoken.

There is nothin', absolutely nothin' you could ever do, no sin big enough, to disqualify you from God's grace.

Always ask yourself this question, "If I heard the mighty thunder roll, and the angel's trumpets blast, would I be saddled up and ready to ride?"

Written by a loving grandfather for his two grandsons, *Things I Wanted My Grandsons to Know Before I Leave* presents a collection of quotes, sayings, snippets, and observations that author Kenn Stobbe believes helped him to live a successful, God-centered life

Kenn's grandsons were born to his only child, an adopted daughter. The boys became the sons the older man never had, both were born when he was already in his sixties. Today, a combination of school, distance, sporting events limits his one on one time to share those things that comprised his moral compass with the boys. Now in his 70's and the winter of his life, Kenn—thinking he would not live long enough to pass any words of wisdom along to his grandsons as they were growing up—decided to write them out instead.

His primary objective is to help his grandsons live the same type of life he has himself. As part of this collection, Kenn addresses, life, love, common sense, manners, morals, values, and beliefs, with a sprinkling of his own thoughts and opinions. Some of the entries are humorous, while others are more serious and thought-provoking.

Things I Wanted My Grandsons to Know Before I Leave offers a heartwarming glimpse into the character and integrity of one man and into the depth of his love for his grandsons.

KENN STOBBE has always admired the cowboy way of life-simple, hardowkring, and honest. He and his wife, Jan, make their home in ranching country northwest of Burwell, Nebraska, in the beautiful Nebraska Sandhills

9 781638 127635